BATTLES OF
LEXINGTON AND CONCORD

BY JOHN HAMILTON

VISIT US AT
WWW.ABDOPUBLISHING.COM

Published by ABDO Publishing Company, PO Box 398166, Minneapolis, MN 55439. Copyright ©2014 by Abdo Consulting Group, Inc. International copyrights reserved in all countries. No part of this book may be reproduced in any form without written permission from the publisher. ABDO & Daughters™ is a trademark and logo of ABDO Publishing Company.

Printed in the United States of America, North Mankato, Minnesota.
112013
012014

 PRINTED ON RECYCLED PAPER

Editor: Sue Hamilton
Graphic Design: Sue Hamilton
Cover Design: Neil Klinepier
Cover Photo: Ken Bohrer
Interior Images: AP-pgs 4, 7, 27, 28 & 29; Corbis-pgs 9, 18 (William Dawes) & 19; Francis Cotes-pg 13 (Francis Smith); Getty Images-pgs 1, 8 & 16; Granger Collection-10, 11 & 12; Historical Image Bank-pgs 15 (bottom), 20, 21 & 24; John Hamilton-pg 22; John Singleton Copley-pgs 13 (Thomas Gage) & 18 (Paul Revere); Ken Bohrer-pgs 14, 17, 23, 25 & 26; Thinkstock-pgs 5 & 6.

ABDO Booklinks
To learn more about Great Battles, visit ABDO Publishing Company online. Web sites about Great Battles are featured on our Booklinks pages. These links are routinely monitored and updated to provide the most current information available. Web site: www.abdopublishing.com

Library of Congress Control Number: 2013946975

Cataloging-in-Publication Data

Hamilton, John, 1959-
 Battles of Lexington and Concord / John Hamilton.
  p. cm. -- (Great battles)
Includes index.
ISBN 978-1-62403-208-0
1. Lexington, Battle of, Lexington, Mass., 1775--Juvenile literature. 2. Concord, Battle of, Concord, Mass., 1775--Juvenile literature.   I. Title.
973.3/311--dc23
                              2013946975

CONTENTS

THE STRUGGLE FOR LIBERTY

A shot rang out at dawn on April 19, 1775. To this day, nobody is 100 percent certain who fired his weapon on the public square in Lexington, Massachusetts. Was it a British Redcoat sent to disarm troublesome American colonists? Or was it a Massachusetts Minuteman defying the authority of the British king? Whoever fired that fateful shot set in motion a string of events that led to the creation of a new nation, and caused dread among the world's tyrants.

The Battles of Lexington and Concord marked the beginning of armed conflict between Great Britain and its American colonies. When an organized group of Patriots fired in unison at crack British troops and drove them from Concord's North Bridge, the event marked the start of war, and so much more. It was "the shot heard 'round the world," according to Ralph Waldo Emerson in his poem "Concord Hymn." What he meant was that the opening skirmishes of the battle weren't simply the beginning of the American Revolutionary War. They marked the start of a struggle for liberty and justice everywhere, traits that are a part of the American soul to this day.

British and Patriot troops fire at a reenactment of the Battle of Concord.

A Minuteman statue in Concord, Massachusetts.

5

THE ROAD TO WAR

King George III and Great Britain's Parliament began taxing American colonists in the 1760s to help pay for the French and Indian War.

In early 1775, Great Britain's colonies in America were a time bomb waiting to explode. The unrest was especially serious in Boston, Massachusetts. The citizens of this major New England port city had suffered for many years. Their misery was the result of a war fought more than 15 years earlier. Called the French and Indian War, it was part of a larger struggle between Great Britain and its arch rival France. By 1760, the British forces of King George III emerged victorious over France and its Native American allies. The British gained much new territory as a result, but it also struggled with a crushing war debt. The Crown's cashboxes were nearly empty, and it needed a quick way to refill them.

King George III and the British Parliament decided that since the American colonies benefitted the most from the British army's victories, it was only fair that the colonies should help pay for the war. Parliament passed a series of taxes on the colonies, including the Sugar Act of 1764, the Stamp Act of 1765, and the Townshend Acts of 1767.

The new taxes caused the cost of goods in America to increase, which led to bitter resentment among the colonists. What was especially infuriating was that the colonists had no representatives in Parliament, nobody to defend their side of the issues. The Americans claimed that only the 13 colonial legislatures had the right to tax the colonists. Therefore, the colonists said, the new British taxes were illegal. "No taxation without representation" became a rallying cry throughout the colonies.

The strong resentment against Great Britain caused radical groups to arise in the colonies. In New England, the Sons of Liberty became very well organized, thanks to leaders such as Samuel Adams and John Hancock, both from Massachusetts. Talk grew of resistance, and even of independence.

American colonists protest the Stamp Act of 1765 in New York City.

7

British soldiers killed three colonists and wounded several others during the 1770 Boston Massacre.

On March 5, 1770, a group of British soldiers in Boston fired on an angry mob of colonists, killing three and wounding several others. The "Boston Massacre" persuaded many colonists to support the Patriot cause.

On the night of December 16, 1773, furious colonists dumped crates of British tea into Boston Harbor. This act of protest became known as the "Boston Tea Party."

It was a reaction to Britain's monopoly on the tea trade, and a major distrust of King George III and Parliament.

For King George III, this act of vandalism was the last straw. In 1774, Parliament passed new laws punishing the unruly American radicals. The laws were called the Coercive Acts, known in the colonies as the Intolerable Acts because they were so hated.

The Boston Tea Party took place on December 16, 1773.

First, Boston Harbor would be closed until the value of the tea was repaid. This was a heavy blow to the people of Boston because much business depended on ships using the busy seaport. British warships soon sailed into the harbor to enforce the closure.

The new laws limited the right of the people of Massachusetts to govern themselves. Boston residents were also forced to house British soldiers in their own homes. This "Quartering Act" was especially hated. In addition, orders were given to arrest leaders of the radical Sons of Liberty.

King George III and Parliament passed the Coercive Acts to punish Massachusetts. The laws were also meant as a warning to the other colonies. But instead of making the colonists afraid to disobey, the unjust rules united the Americans against Great Britain. Throughout the colonies, talk of revolution was in the air. On March 23, 1775, attorney Patrick Henry addressed the Virginia House of Burgesses. In a fiery speech, Henry declared that the time for war was at hand. "I know not what course others may take," Henry said, "but as for me, give me liberty or give me death!"

LEADERS OF THE
PATRIOTS

Samuel Adams (1722-1803) was a radical Patriot who had a talent for stirring things up. Born in Boston, Massachusetts, he was highly educated, graduating from Harvard College in 1740. He was an unsuccessful businessman before becoming a politician and philosopher. Adams opposed British tax policies imposed on the colonies. He believed that Parliament's actions were against the law. Adams wrote that the American colonists should have every right granted to any English person. He argued that the new taxes violated the British constitution.

Samuel Adams

Adams was skilled at organizing political protests. He organized secret radical groups such as the Sons of Liberty and the Committees of Correspondence. He also organized the protest that led to the Boston Tea Party in 1773. Shortly before the Battles of Lexington and Concord in 1775, the British ordered that Adams be arrested for treason. Warned of the threat, Adams escaped to Philadelphia, Pennsylvania.

After years of protest, Adams began to believe that the only real solution to America's problems was independence. Adams strongly urged his fellow colonists to break away from Great Britain. He was a member of the First and Second Continental Congress, and was a signer of the Declaration of Independence. After the revolution, Adams served as governor of Massachusetts from 1794 to 1797.

John Hancock

John Hancock (1737-1793) was a successful Boston businessman who earned his wealth in the shipping industry. He spent much of his money on projects that benefitted the public, which made him very popular. His anti-British political activities, however, made him a wanted man. He escaped with fellow Patriot Samuel Adams during the Battles of Lexington and Concord on April 19, 1775.

Hancock was very involved in Massachusetts politics, which led to his election as president of the Second Continental Congress in Philadelphia, Pennsylvania, in May 1775. As president, Hancock became the first signer of the Declaration of Independence on July 4, 1776. His large signature is famous today.

Joseph Warren

Dr. Joseph Warren (1741-1775) was a surgeon and Boston politician who frequently met with fellow Patriots Samuel Adams and John Hancock. Warren served as president of the Massachusetts Provincial Congress, a very high position in the rebel government. Warren often gave speeches and wrote newspaper articles critical of British policies. It was Warren who sent Paul Revere and William Dawes into the countryside on the night of April 18, 1775, to warn of a British attack. He fought the next day during the Battles of Lexington and Concord. Warren was killed the following month during the Battle of Bunker Hill.

LEADERS OF GREAT
BRITAIN

King George III (1738-1820) ruled Great Britain for almost 60 years, from 1760 to 1820. His subjects in Great Britain loved him, but in America he was a hated tyrant who punished anyone who disobeyed his orders, no matter how unfair. Before his reign, taxes and regulations on trade goods with the American colonies were often not enforced. George III was determined to change that. His strict policies meant that Americans were taxed, even though they didn't have a voice in the British government.

King George III

George III continually ignored the colonists's objections to being taxed and regulated without representation in Parliament. The king, however, insisted that the colonists must obey his rule. His harsh policies led to the American Revolution. In his later years, George III suffered from mental illness that may have been caused by a disease called porphyria. His son, George IV, took over most of his duties in 1811.

Thomas Gage

General Thomas Gage (1720–1787) was the commander of British forces in North America at the start of the American Revolution in 1775. He was also the military governor of Massachusetts. He earlier fought during the French and Indian War, and proved his administrative abilities while serving as the military governor of the city of Montreal, Canada. In 1763, Gage became the official commander-in-chief of all British forces in North America.

Having spent so many years in the colonies, Gage believed he knew Americans very well. He felt sympathy for their problems, and even married a woman from New Jersey. But Gage was a British military officer, with total loyalty first and foremost to King George III. By 1775, rebellion was looming. Gage tried to control the unrest by strictly enforcing British law. His attempt to seize illegal weapons from colonial militias sparked the Battles of Lexington and Concord, which marked the beginning of the war. After the disastrous British defeat at the Battle of Bunker Hill, Gage was replaced by Sir William Howe.

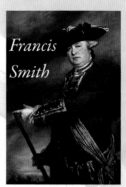

Francis Smith

Lieutenant Colonel Francis Smith (1723-1791) commanded the British troops that clashed with American militia forces during the Battles of Lexington and Concord. Smith was overweight and slow to react, but he could also display courage in battle. Smith's orders from General Gage were to destroy rebel weapons, but not to hurt the colonists or plunder their possessions. Smith was assisted by **Major John Pitcairn** (1722-1775), of the Royal Marines. Both Smith and Pitcairn have been criticized for being unable to fully control their troops, which led to the battle that started the American Revolution.

TACTICS AND WEAPONS

Up close and personal: that was the style of most fighting during the American Revolution. The majority of firearms, including flintlock muskets and pistols, had smooth bores and did not fire accurately at long distances. Usually, soldiers looked into the faces of their opponents before firing their weapons. And because it took so long to reload, troops often resorted to close-quarter fighting with bayonets, swords, and axes.

Because their firearms were so inaccurate, the standard military procedure was to arrange troops in a line standing shoulder to shoulder. When an officer gave the order, they fired a volley of shots all at once, sending a deadly mass of lead balls toward the enemy. After a row of soldiers fired, they stepped backward and a second row took their place, allowing the first row time to reload.

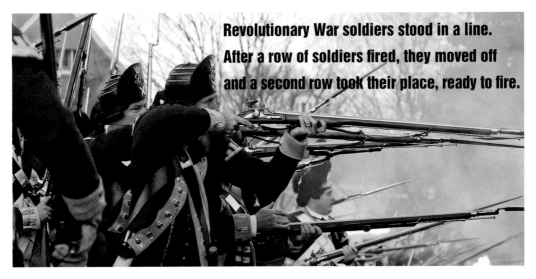

Revolutionary War soldiers stood in a line. After a row of soldiers fired, they moved off and a second row took their place, ready to fire.

Brown Bess

Charleville

Even though the muskets were inaccurate, troops on the front line were especially exposed, and many were inevitably struck down.

The most common firearms were the Brown Bess and Charleville smoothbore muskets. These were used against targets about 80-100 yards (73-91 m) away. Some troops were armed with rifles, which had spiral grooves inside the barrels that made bullets spin and travel more accurately.

Artillery such as cannons and mortars were often used to defend and defeat forts. Smaller field cannons could kill dozens of enemy troops at once.

A British Army Royal Artillery Gunner stands guard next to a cannon.

THE MIDNIGHT RIDERS

In April 1775, British General Thomas Gage, the military governor of Massachusetts, had a big problem. Talk of rebellion was in the air, and many people in the American colonies were beginning to arm themselves. In Massachusetts, groups of citizen-soldiers were training themselves in military tactics. These men, who were mostly farmers and shopkeepers, called themselves the Minutemen. They pledged to be ready to fight at a moment's notice if the British continued violating the colonists's freedom. They secretly stored weapons, gunpowder, and supplies in houses and farms in rural areas. General Gage was determined to find these weapons and destroy them to keep the peace.

The Old North Church

On the night of April 18, 1775, Gage sent out a military unit of about 700 troops from the city of Boston. There were rumors of a rebel weapons stockpile in the town of Concord, about 20 miles (32 km) west of Boston. The village of Lexington was about halfway between Boston and Concord.

Gage ordered his men to secretly march in the middle of the night to Concord and seize any Patriot weapons and supplies they could find. They were also to arrest rebel leaders Samuel Adams and John Hancock, who were rumored to be in the area. The Redcoats would first board boats and take a shortcut across the Charles River, then march along the road to Lexington and Concord.

Actors recreate the march from Boston to Concord by British troops.

17

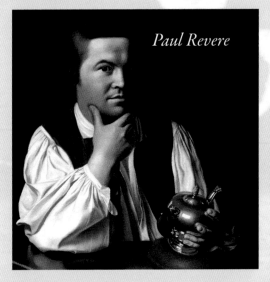
Paul Revere

William Dawes

Dr. Joseph Warren was another Patriot leader wanted by the British. Warren was in Boston when rebel spies told him that Redcoats were on their way to Concord. He enlisted the help of couriers Paul Revere and William Dawes. Their mission was to ride west by horseback to warn Adams, Hancock, and others that the British were coming.

Revere was a successful Boston silversmith who became active in anti-British politics. He spied on British soldiers, and took part in the Boston Tea Party. On the night of April 18, Revere arranged for two lanterns to be placed in Boston's Old North Church tower. It was a signal to other Patriots in the area about the British troop movements ("One if by land, two if by sea," according to the famous poem by Henry Wadsworth Longfellow, "Paul Revere's Ride").

The British were unaware that the Americans had already moved most of their weapons out of Concord, having been warned days earlier of an impending British attack. But Patriot leaders Adams and Hancock were hiding at the home of Hancock's relatives in Lexington, and were in danger of being swept up in the British dragnet. They had to be warned.

Revere and Dawes slipped out of the city and took different routes, warning as many citizens as they could that British soldiers were heading toward Concord. Revere narrowly evaded a British patrol just outside Charlestown, Massachusetts. He then continued his midnight ride, warning Patriot militias in nearby towns along the way.

In the early morning hours of April 19, both Revere and Dawes rode into Lexington. They warned Adams and Hancock of the approaching danger (both Patriot leaders escaped to Philadelphia, Pennsylvania).

Revere and Dawes, now joined by another rebel courier, Samuel Prescott, continued on the road to Concord. They were stopped by a British patrol.

Prescott and Dawes escaped, but Revere was captured. Dawes was later bucked off his horse and could not continue, but Prescott made it all the way to Concord in time to warn the Minutemen of the approaching British soldiers.

Revere was questioned by the British, and later released. The damage had already been done: the secret British attack on Concord was no longer a secret. All up and down the Lexington-Concord road, Patriot militia troops were beginning to gather.

At dawn, after a long night's march, the British troops arrived in Lexington. The first clash of the American Revolution was about to begin.

On the night of April 18, 1775, couriers Revere and Dawes warned citizens that the British were coming.

THE FIRST CLASH AT
LEXINGTON

As the sun rose on April 19, 1775, Captain John Parker of the Lexington militia stood with about 70 troops on a flat area of ground, a sort of village park called Lexington Green. The area overlooked the road leading west to Concord. Despite the danger, Parker wanted to display the Patriots's resolve. He ordered his men to show defiance when the British arrived. "Stand your ground," Parker said. "Don't fire unless fired upon, but if they mean to have a war, let it begin here."

Lexington militiamen gather to meet advancing British soldiers in 1775.

American militia under attack by British Redcoats at Lexington Green.

Soon, hundreds of Redcoats came marching up the road. Under the command of Lieutenant Colonel Francis Smith, and assisted by Major John Pitcairn, a company of British troops went into battle formation and faced the rebel line. Pitcairn called out to the Patriots on the green, "Lay down your arms, you rebels, and disperse!"

Captain Parker knew he was heavily outnumbered. Attacking the British would be suicide. He called out for his men to go back to their homes. Slowly, the rebels followed their orders. But then a shot rang out. Nobody is sure which side fired first, but soon the British troops began firing at will at the Patriots. They then surged forward and attacked with bayonets. When the smoke cleared, eight Massachusetts men were dead, and 10 were wounded. One Redcoat was slightly wounded.

Colonel Smith arrived on the scene and restored order among his men. The British fired a single victory volley into the air, and then reformed their column and continued the march toward Concord.

THE BATTLE AT
CONCORD

After the skirmish in Lexington, the British expedition continued its march to Concord, a distance of about six miles (10 km). They arrived in town between 7:00 and 8:00 a.m. They were watched closely by local militia, who stood ready on the outskirts of town and from a ridge lining the road. The leader of the militia was Colonel James Barrett. He urged his fellow Patriots to be cautious.

The British soldiers arrived in Concord and spread out, securing the roads and bridges into town. Lieutenant Colonel Francis Smith directed his men in carrying out General Gage's orders. Redcoats moved from house to house, searching for hidden weapons and supplies. They discovered musket ammunition and barrels of flour and salted food, which were tossed into a local pond. They also uncovered three large cannons buried in a yard. Smith had their mounts smashed, and their carriages burned.

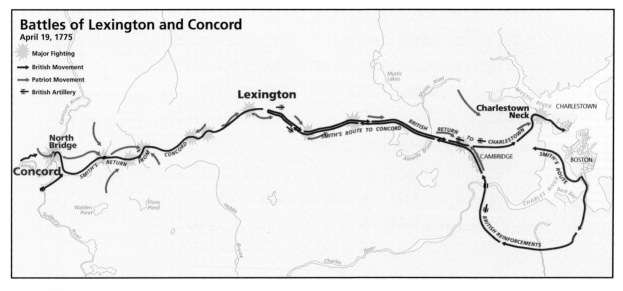

Battles of Lexington and Concord
April 19, 1775

- Major Fighting
- → British Movement
- → Patriot Movement
- British Artillery

North Bridge

Concord

Lexington

Charlestown Neck · CHARLESTOWN

CAMBRIDGE

BOSTON

SMITH'S ROUTE TO CONCORD

BRITISH RETURN TO CHARLESTOWN

SMITH'S RETURN FROM CONCORD

BRITISH REINFORCEMENTS

Patriot militiamen gather and prepare to battle the Redcoats.

Having been warned of fighting in Lexington, militiamen continued to pour in from the surrounding area to defend Concord. About 400 Patriots gathered on high ground above North Bridge, which spanned the Concord River. The bridge was closely guarded by a company of Redcoats numbering about 90 men. The town militiamen, led by Major John Buttrick, watched in horror as smoke began rising from Concord (the result of the cannon carriages being burned). Many mistakenly believed the British were setting fire to the entire town.

Minutemen fire on British troops at Concord's North Bridge.

Major Buttrick ordered his men to move in an organized line toward North Bridge. The British fell back to the opposite side of the bridge and scrambled into a defensive formation. Tension rose to an extreme level as the two sides faced off against each other.

A shot rang out, almost certainly from the British side. It was probably fired by a scared, exhausted Redcoat, but we may never know. The result was that the remaining British troops believed the order had been give to fire upon the rebels. A volley of musket fire filled the air, killing two militiamen on the opposite side.

Major Buttrick hollered for his men to shoot back. "Fire, fellow soldiers, for God's sake, fire!" For several minutes the two sides traded volleys. The British were shocked at the Patriots's well-organized and disciplined attack. They had little respect for these Minutemen. The rebels, after all, were mostly farmers and shopkeepers. The British considered the enemy to be mere rabble, undisciplined, and unskilled in warfare. Much to their surprise, the Concord militia was proving to be a force to be reckoned with.

Soon, the King's soldiers were driven back into town. They were forced to abandon the bodies of three dead Redcoat officers, plus eight wounded. After fleeing in panic, they rejoined the main British force. The victorious militiamen took control of North Bridge. Their total casualties from the skirmish: two dead and three wounded.

By midday, hundreds of additional armed Patriots surrounded the town. Lieutenant Colonel Francis Smith knew his Redcoats would soon be outnumbered. It was time to return to Boston—and quickly.

A reenactment of the British and Patriot soldiers's conflict at the North Bridge.

THE RETREAT TO
CHARLESTOWN

As the British retreated east toward their Boston base, they were shot at from all sides by colonial militia. The rebels used trees and low stone fences as cover, popping up to get off a shot and then ducking down again to reload. Some of the militia were more organized, firing off simultaneous volleys at the fleeing Redcoats.

Lieutenant Colonel Smith sent cavalry troops to counterattack the Patriots and protect the infantry's flanks (sides) as they marched along the road. As they passed Lexington, they were ambushed by even more rebels, many of whom had fought earlier that morning in town. The surprise attack killed several troops and wounded many others. Smith was struck in the thigh. Major John Pitcairn had his horse shot out from under him.

Patriot troops used trees and low stone fences as cover against the Redcoats.

British troops retreating under fire from colonial militia after the Battles of Concord and Lexington.

The British were on the verge of destruction. Many men panicked and ran. But then, help arrived. Led by Lord Hugh Percy, a group of about 1,000 British troops reinforced Lieutenant Colonel Smith's exhausted men. Percy's relief force also included artillery. The two cannons gave the British covering fire, which saved them from being totally wiped out. The final sprint to Boston, however, was a disaster for the British.

For the rest of the day, the outnumbered Redcoats fought a running battle as they hurried back down the road. Everywhere they turned, they were shot at by thousands of angry rebel militiamen. The British burned several houses and inns as they moved along, further infuriating the Patriots. As Smith and Percy led their troops toward safety, rebels continued to pop up from behind fences and trees, picking off the Redcoats one by one. The retreat from Concord turned out to be the bloodiest part of the entire day.

THE BATTLE'S AFTERMATH

By nightfall, the British staggered back into Charlestown, across the harbor from Boston. There, they were protected by reinforcements and the powerful cannons of British warships. At the end of the day's battle, the British suffered 73 dead and about 200 wounded or missing. The Patriots counted 49 dead and 45 wounded or missing.

The morning after the battle, on April 20, 1775, the British woke to find themselves surrounded by at least 7,000 rebel militiamen from Massachusetts and other colonies. Boston was under siege. The British commanders, including General Gage, were in shock. They had vastly underestimated the Patriots's will to fight.

British troops suffered at the hands of the Patriot militiamen at the Battles of Lexington and Concord.

General George Washington took command of Patriot forces surrounding Boston, Massachusetts. The British evacuated the city in March 1776.

The Battles of Lexington and Concord sparked open warfare between the colonies and Great Britain. Although the fighting wasn't as epic as battles yet to come, it served several purposes. The bloodshed caused many colonists to support the struggle for freedom. The style of fighting used by the rebels, a kind of guerrilla warfare that was alien to the British troops, demoralized the Redcoats. The clash at Lexington and Concord proved that the British army was not invincible.

In the weeks and months ahead, thousands more rebel militiamen continued their stranglehold on Boston until, by March 1776, the British were forced to flee the city by ship. It was the Patriots's first major campaign victory. There were many long years left to fight, but the struggle for an independent United States of America was well on its way.

GLOSSARY

ACT

A law or regulation.

ARTILLERY

Large weapons of war, such as cannons, mortars, and howitzers, that are used by military forces on land and at sea to hurl explosive projectiles at the enemy.

CAVALRY

During the American Revolution era, soldiers who rode and fought on horseback were called cavalry. Modern cavalry includes soldiers who fight in armored vehicles such as tanks or attack helicopters.

COLONY

A group of people who settle in a distant territory but remain citizens of their native country.

FLINTLOCK

A weapon such as a musket, rifle, or pistol, which is fired using the flintlock system created in the early 1600s. When the firearm's trigger is pulled, a hammer with a flint tip strikes a metal plate, causing a spark. This spark ignites the gunpowder inside the barrel. The resulting explosion forces the lead ball-shaped bullet out of the barrel.

HOUSE OF BURGESSES

An assembly of elected representatives in Virginia that passed laws and regulations.

MILITIA

Citizens who were part-time soldiers rather than professional army fighters. Militiamen, such as the Minutemen from Massachusetts, usually fought only in their local areas and continued with their normal jobs when they were not needed.

MONOPOLY

Complete control over the production and sales of a product or service.

PARLIAMENT

The law-making body of Great Britain. It consists of the House of Lords and the House of Commons.

PATRIOTS

Colonists who rebelled against Great Britain during the American Revolution.

RADICALS

Colonists who were strongly opposed to the policies of Great Britain.

REDCOATS

The name that was often given to British soldiers because part of their uniform included a bright red coat.

REVOLUTION

A sudden, sweeping change in government.

SMOOTHBORE

Smoothbore weapons are constructed with barrels—the part the bullet travels down—that are smooth on the inside. When the weapon is fired, the loose-fitting ammunition bounces from side to side until it emerges from the barrel. The bullet's motion greatly decreases the weapon's accuracy.

SONS OF LIBERTY

A group of Patriot colonists who banded together to oppose the Stamp Act, Townshend Acts, and other oppressive laws imposed by Great Britain.

INDEX